cut on broken lines and place tab
behind face

attach paper strips to back
of dress

New York debut

Plate 2

Aunt Alicia's ball gown

Plate 3

place tab behind face

attach paper strips to back
of dress

Sailing for England

**Plate 4**

do not cut out white space
between arm and body

attach paper strip to back of skirt

do not cut out white space
between riding crop and skirt

Riding at Blenheim Palace

**Plate 5**

attach paper strip to back of skirt

Writing letters

**Plate 6**

cut on broken line and place tab
behind face

Channel crossing

Plate 7

attach paper strip to back of skirt

Dinner in Paris

Plate 8

cut on broken line and place tab
behind face

attach paper strip to back of skirt

Shopping at Maison Worth

Plate 9

attach paper strip to back of skirt

Afternoon tea

**Plate 10**

Skating in Bavaria

**Plate 11**

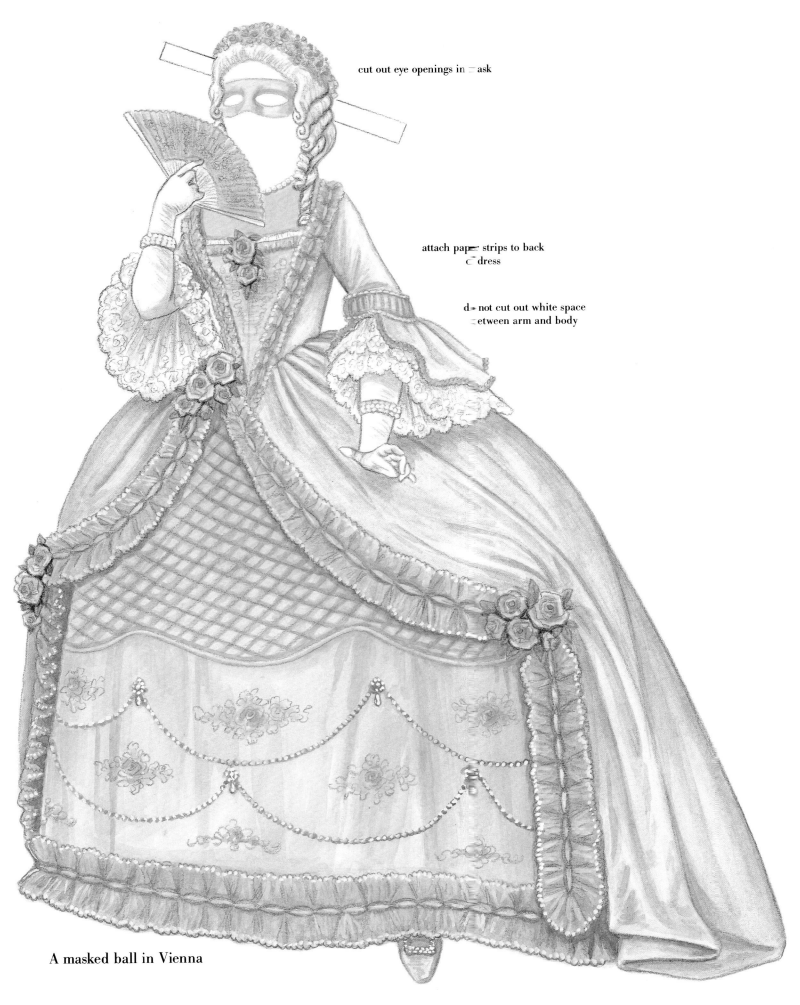

cut out eye openings in mask

attach paper strips to back
of dress

do not cut out white space
between arm and body

A masked ball in Vienna

**Plate 12**

Afternoon "at home"

Plate 13

cut or broken line and place tab
behind face

Walking tour of Venice

**Plate 14**

cut on broken line and place tab
behind face

attach paper strips to back
of costume

Fiesta in Madrid

**Plate 15**

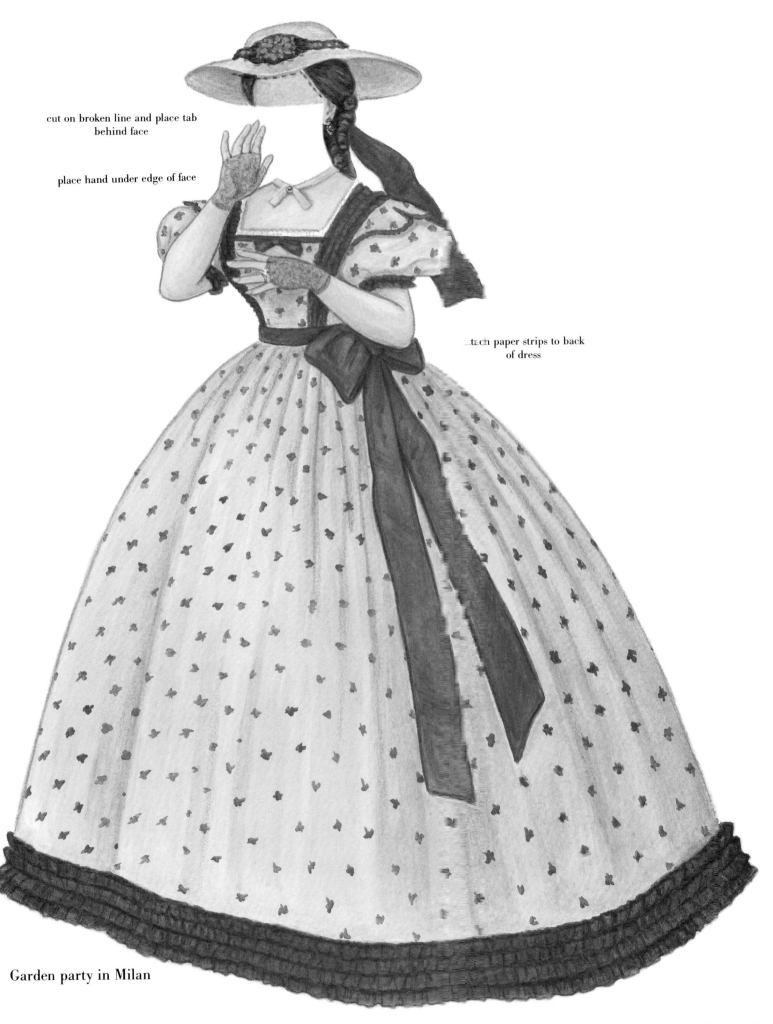

cut on broken line and place tab
behind face

place hand under edge of face

attach paper strips to back
of dress

Garden party in Milan

Plate 16

cut on broken line and place tab
behind face

attach paper strips to back
of dress

Wedding in New York

Plate 17

Aunt Alicia

Plate 18